Art In America

Kevin Long
Copyright © 2017 Author Name

All rights reserved.

ISBN-13: 978-1979954839
ISBN-10: 1979954836

For a long time Art lived in Paris. Then there was a war and it was not safe for Art to stay there anymore. A woman named Peggy was kind enough to help Art escape Paris, and introduced Art to other people who had also escaped.

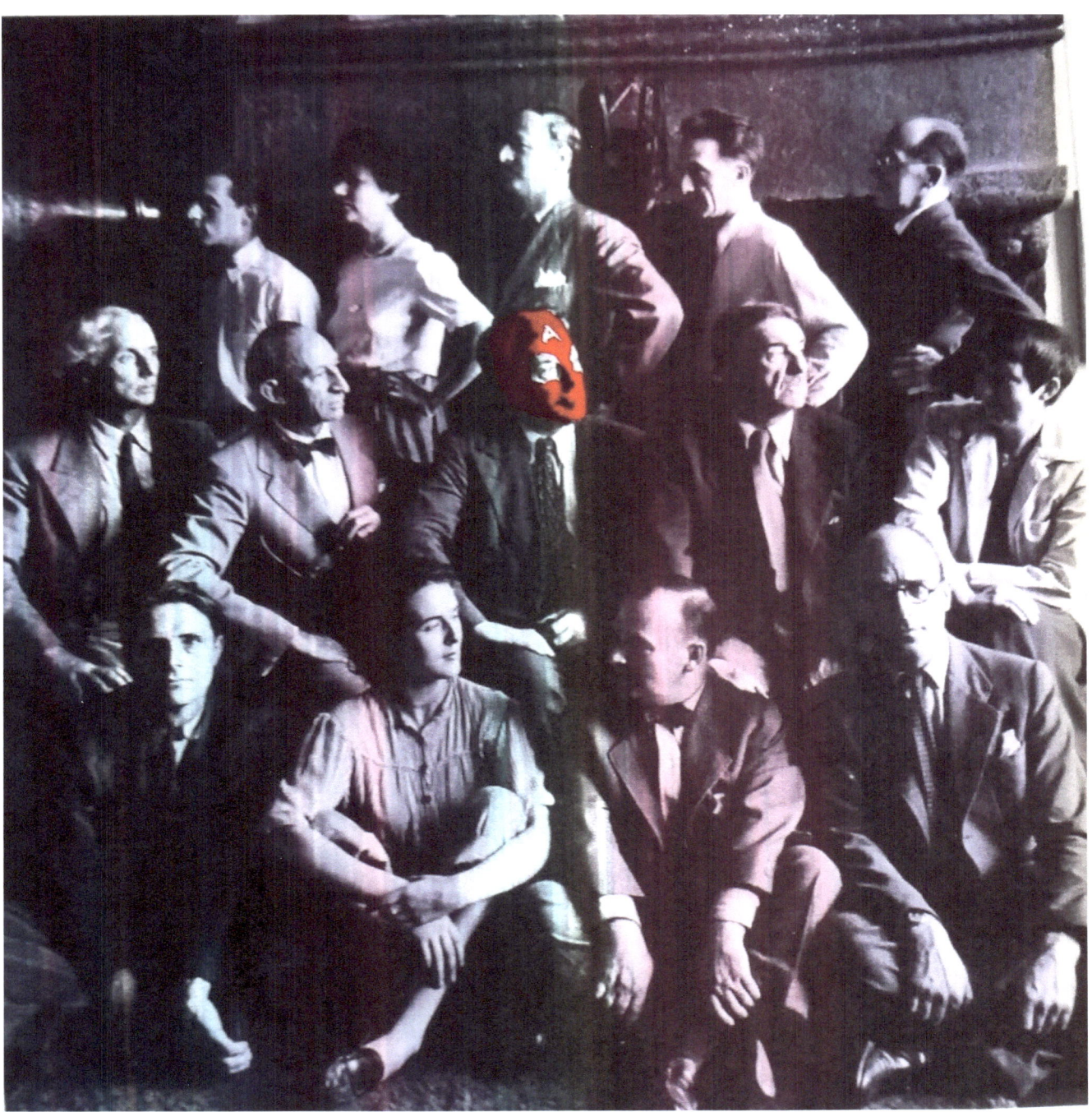

Art arrived in this new place ready to make something. Art was very creative and full of ideas.

Art wanted to make something that was different, something that was exciting. But Art was also full of existential dread. The painting would be a stunning record of being there and alive. Art began dancing in the studio flinging, dripping, and stabbing paint at the canvas.

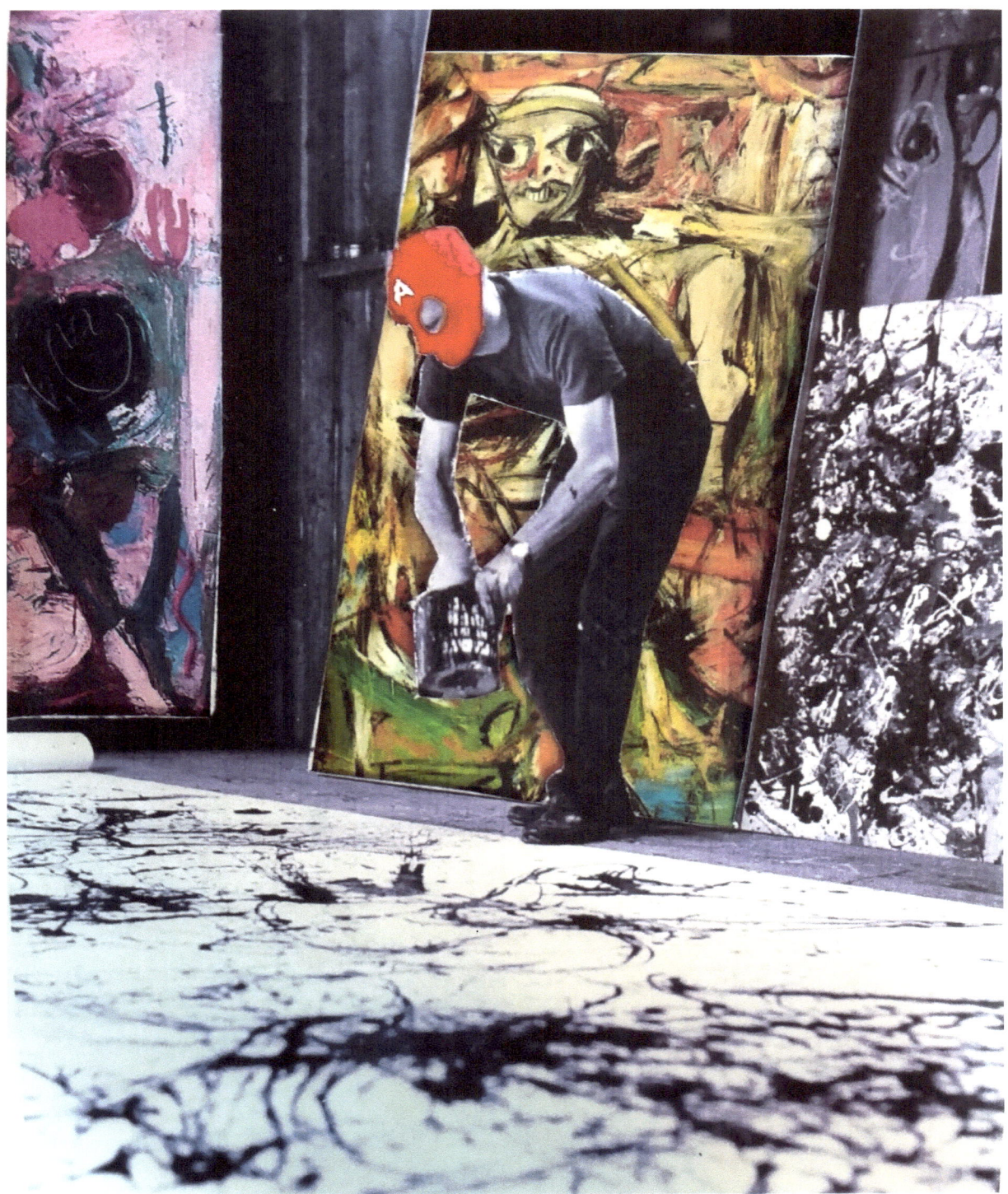

People loved the paintings, especially a man named Clement. "This is pure painting!" he proclaimed. "2 dimensionality guarantees painting's independence as an art!" he said. Art found this a bit confusing, but agreed with him. Art began to make paintings that celebrated how flat the canvas could be, and the tricks that could play on your eyes.

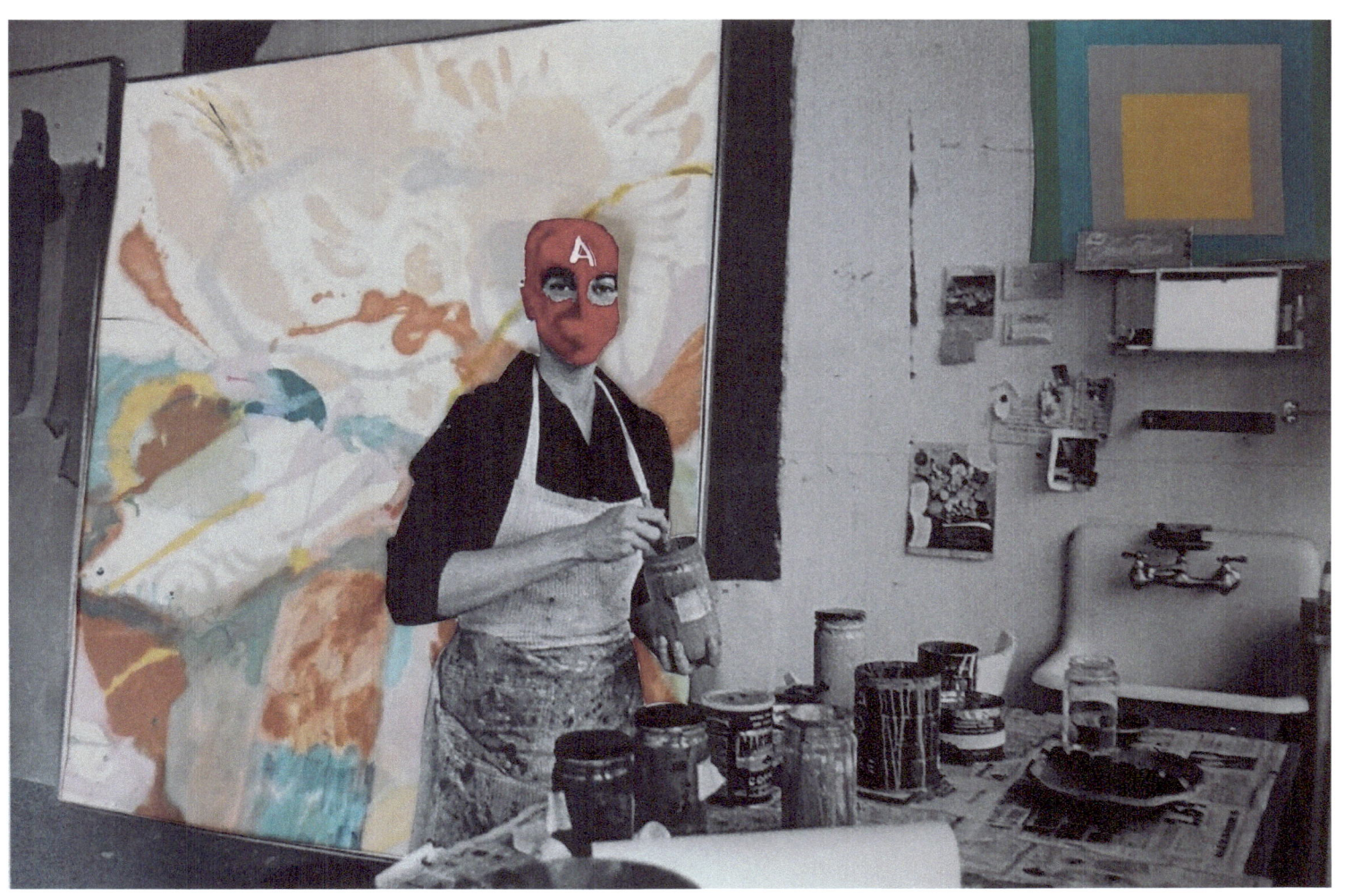

Art began to think. Everything is going by so fast. What if I can make people slow down. To sit and just look at something for a minute, maybe even 5 minutes. "If they did that," Art thought, "then they might view the world a little differently"

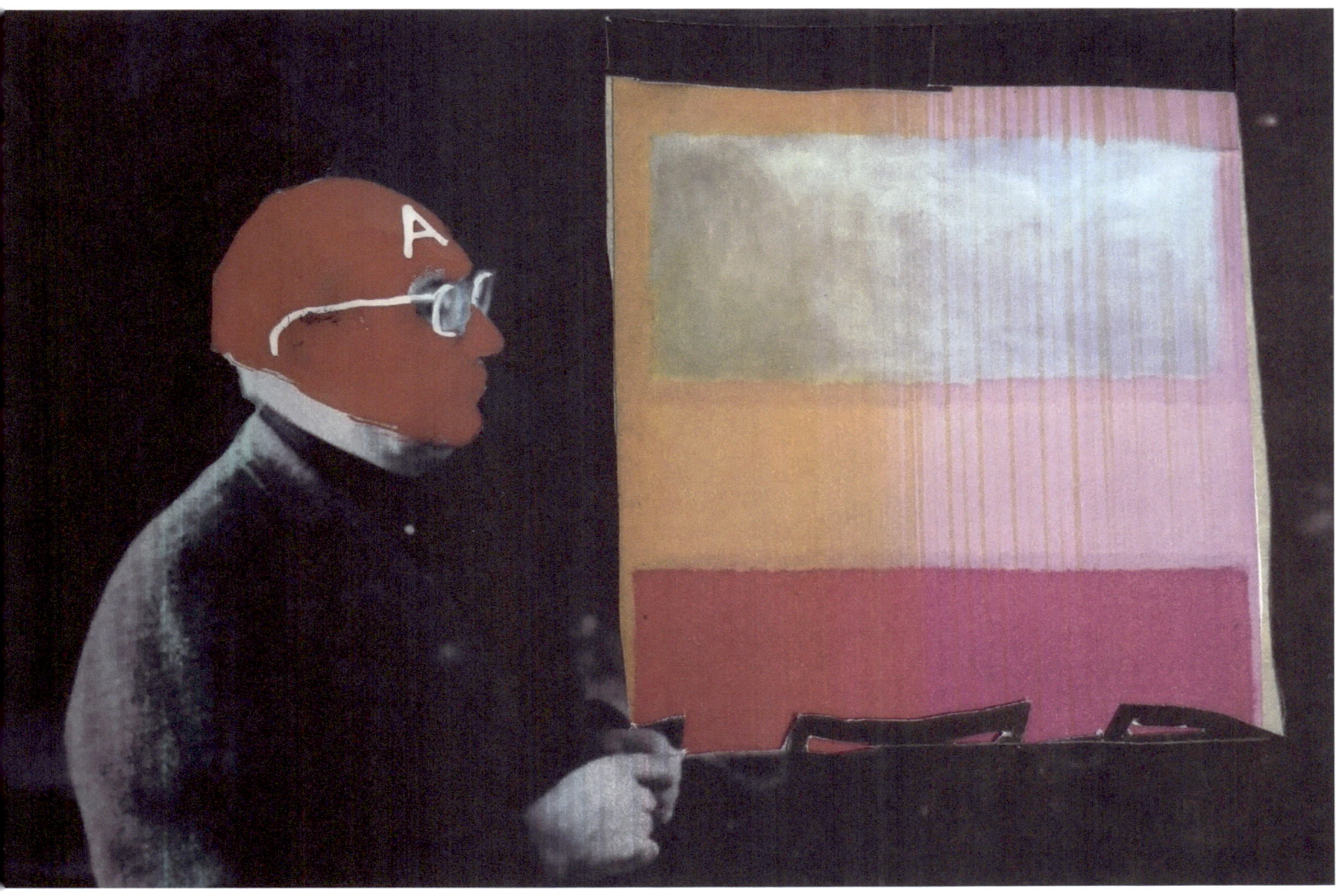

Art began to look at things a little differently too. Art noticed that by looking at things investigating them deep enough, their beauty would come out. "What if beauty exists all around us?" Art thought. So Art tried to make other people aware of the beauty around them too. So one day Art got a whole group of people into an auditorium and sat in front of a piano for 4 minutes and 33 seconds. The audience sat too, and listened to all the sounds they usually ignored.

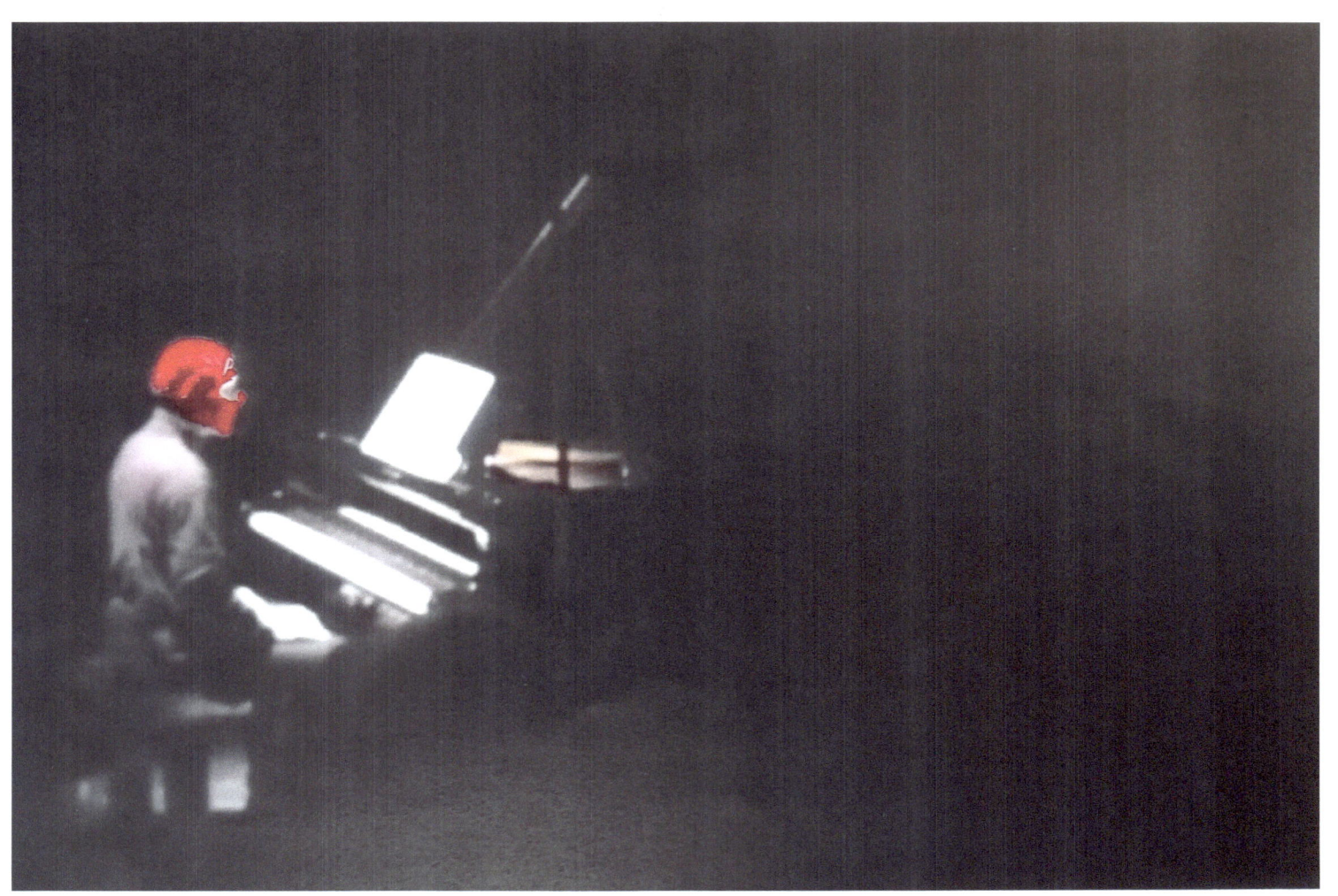

Art began to think about the things people usually ignore. There were piles of newspapers and magazines full of pictures. There was a pile of junk in front of every house on garbage day. There were stores and houses full of things to be explored and seen. Art began to collect images and objects that would otherwise be thrown out or ignored. "What if I used everything I do to create?" Art thought.

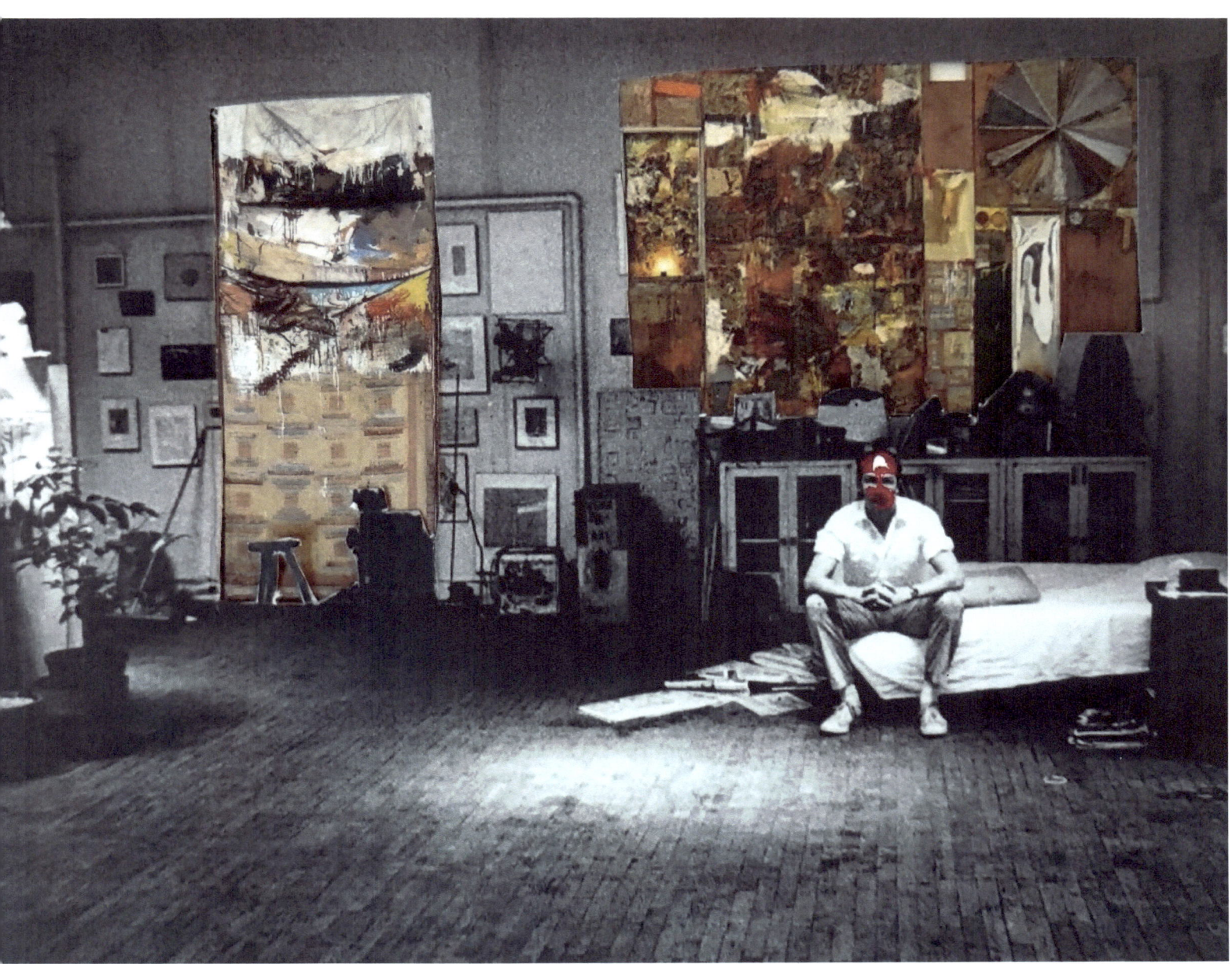

Art really started looking at the world very closely. At the store, Art saw shelves full of bright packaging going way to the left and right and up almost to the ceiling. On TV, Art saw famous people over and over again, but learned very little about them. "What if we are all the same, just like the boxes and cans on the shelf?" Art thought, "This could be interesting."

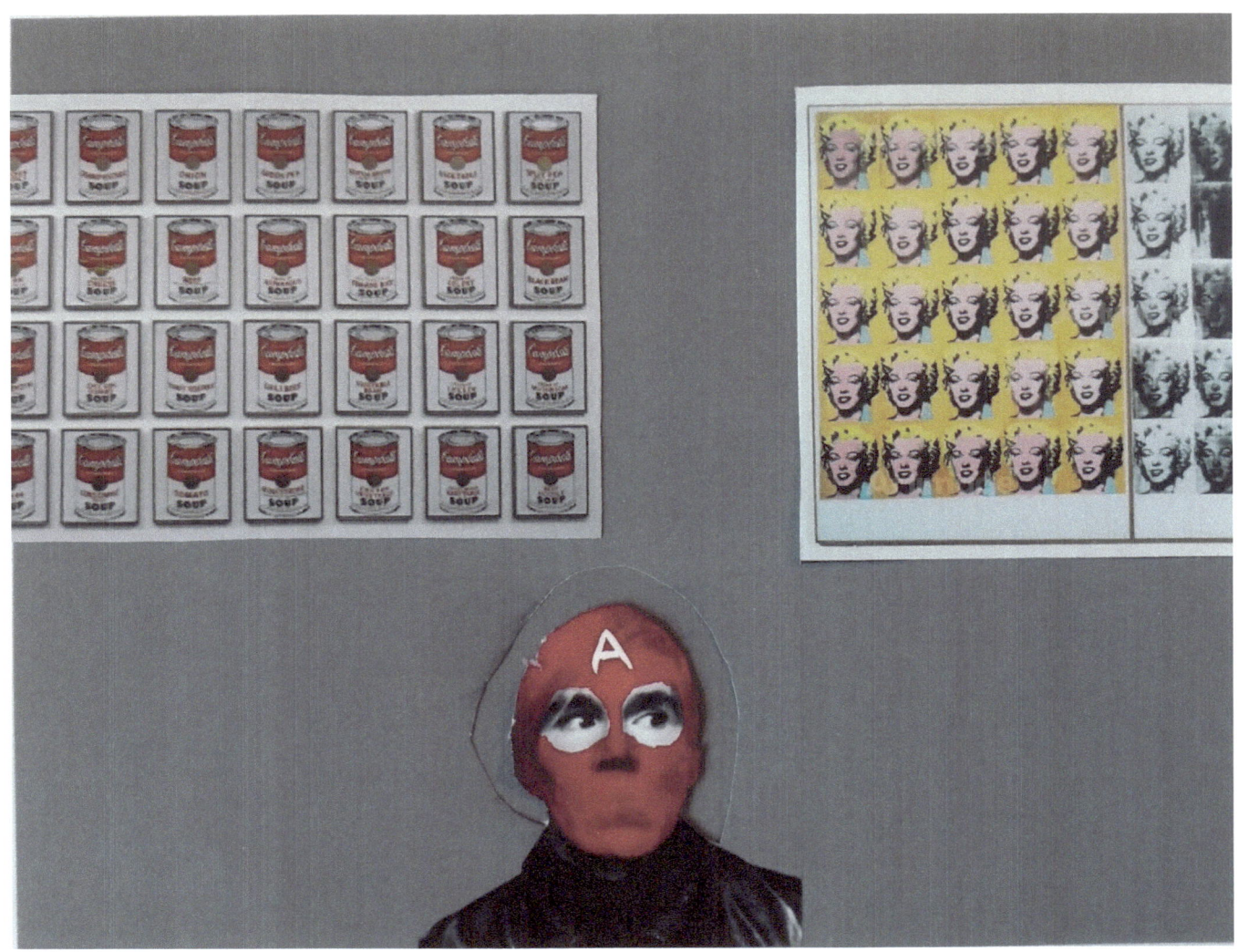

After seeing beauty everywhere, Art now started to see the beauty was fleeting. Art only saw shapes and materials. People stared into the objects and felt nothing. The objects were empty and so were the people.

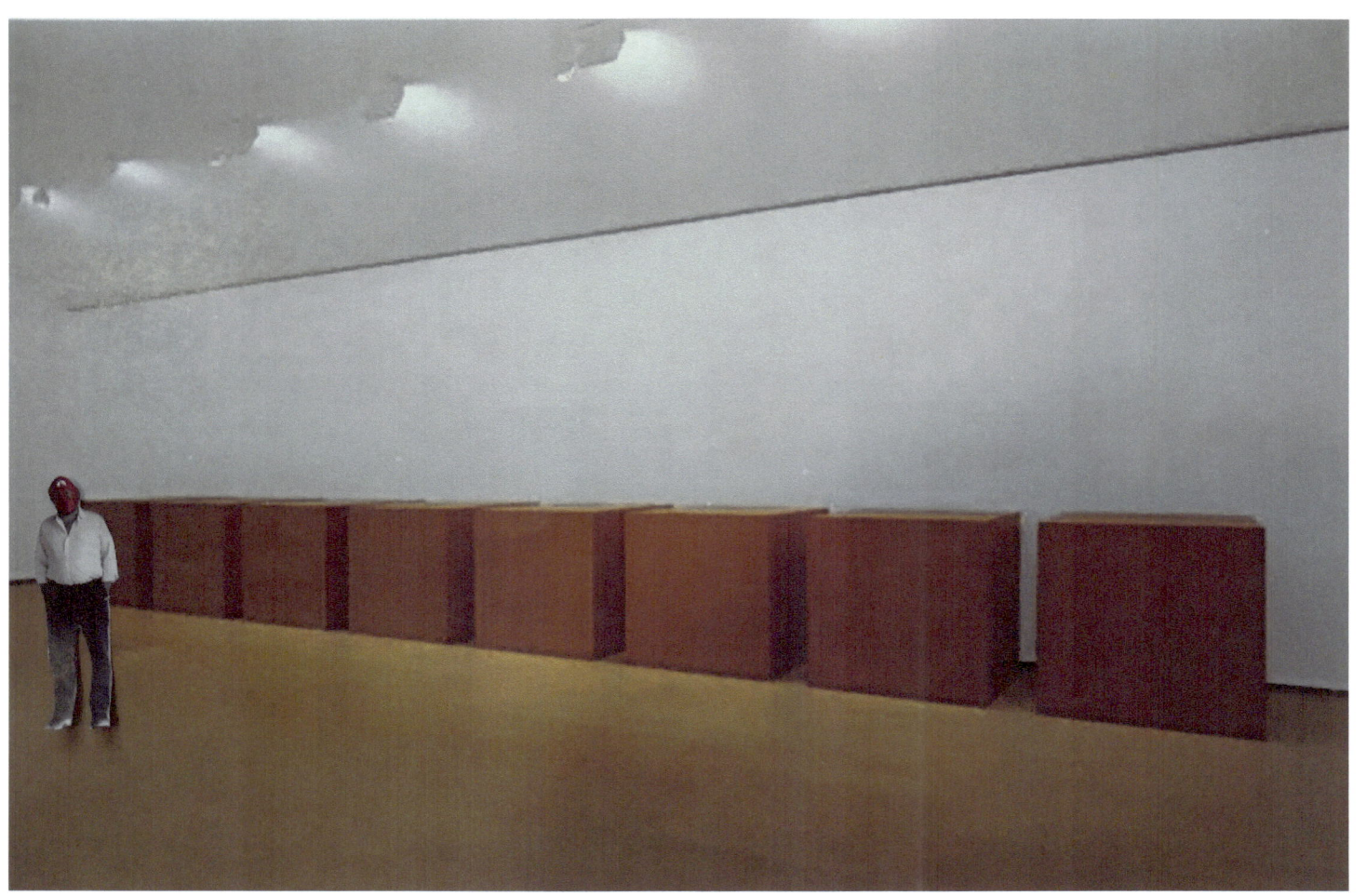

Art decided to use the space around the objects too. Beauty would be the sculpture and the hills and the people and their conversations and work they do to create. It would not matter if they were temporary as long as they made people think and see the world differently. Not everyone was ready to think and see differently. Art made the work anyway.

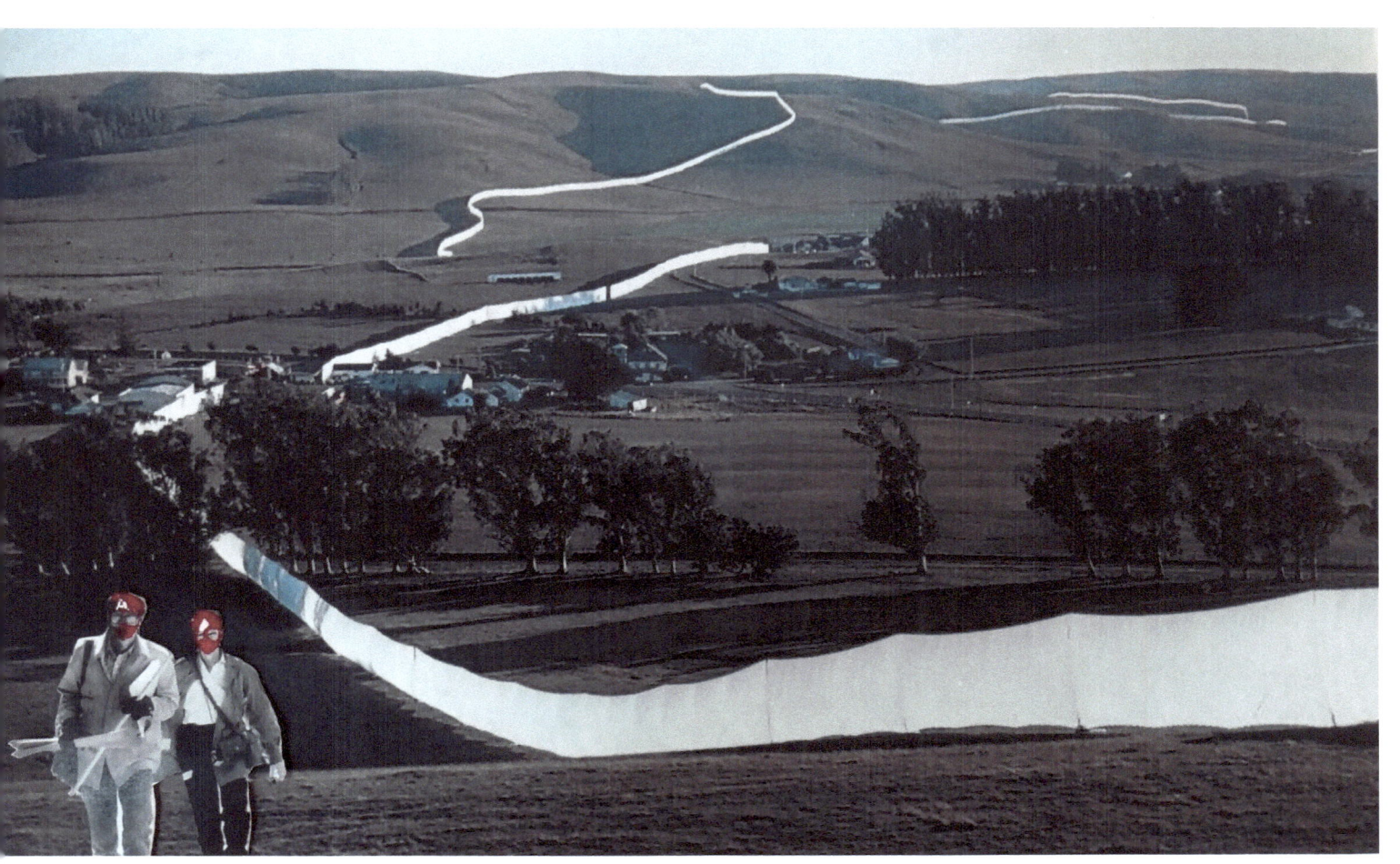

Art looked back on all the beauty created. Art had done so much, there can't be any more new ideas. Then Art realized that not everyone's voice had been heard, and not everyone was listening. There was so much more of the world to explore. There is no end to new ideas, new stories to be told, new images to create as long as you are willing to look, and listen.

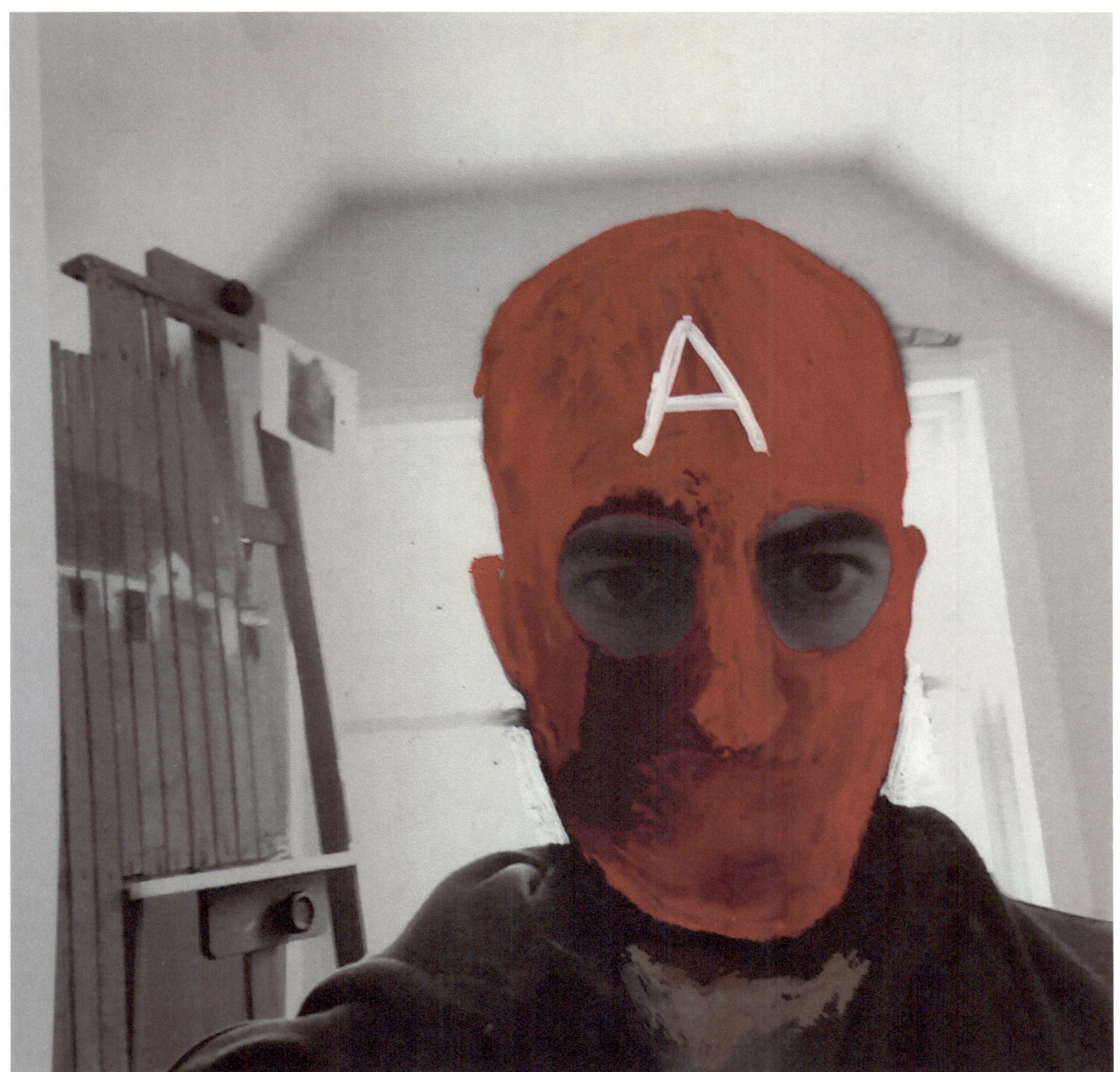

Glossary of Artists

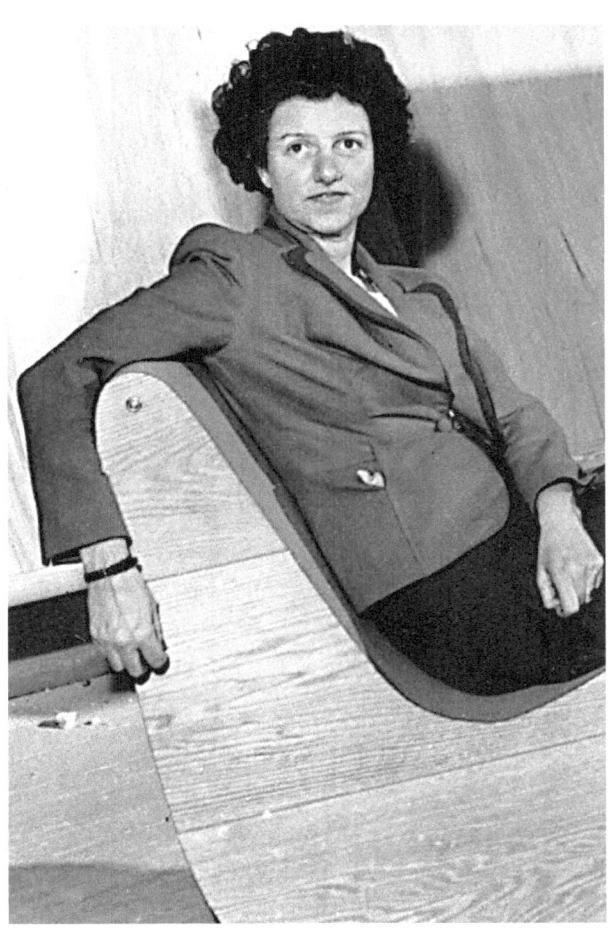

Peggy Guggenheim (1898-1979) was an American art collector. She lived in France up until the beginning of World War II and escaped just before the Germans took Paris. When she returned to New York her gallery *Art of this Century* and her apartment were gathering spaces for the artists she had befriended while in Europe. She helped them integrate into the New York Art scene, and in the process fostered a dialogue between the European artists and the younger generation of artists already living in New York.

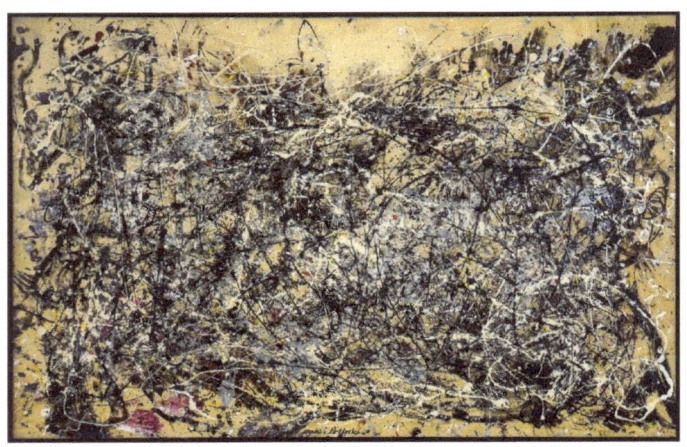

Jackson Pollock
Number 1 1948
Oil on canvas 1948

Jackson Pollock (1912-1956) was an American artist who worked mainly in New York. His dripped and splattered paintings challenged the ideas of what a painting was and brought him great fame in the 1940's and 50's. Pollock's work is indicative of the "all over" composition, where the image is seemingly uniformly distributed across the canvas. His work records what was described as his dance around and above the canvas. Pollock wanted his viewer to "not look for, but look passively and try to receive what the painting has to offer."

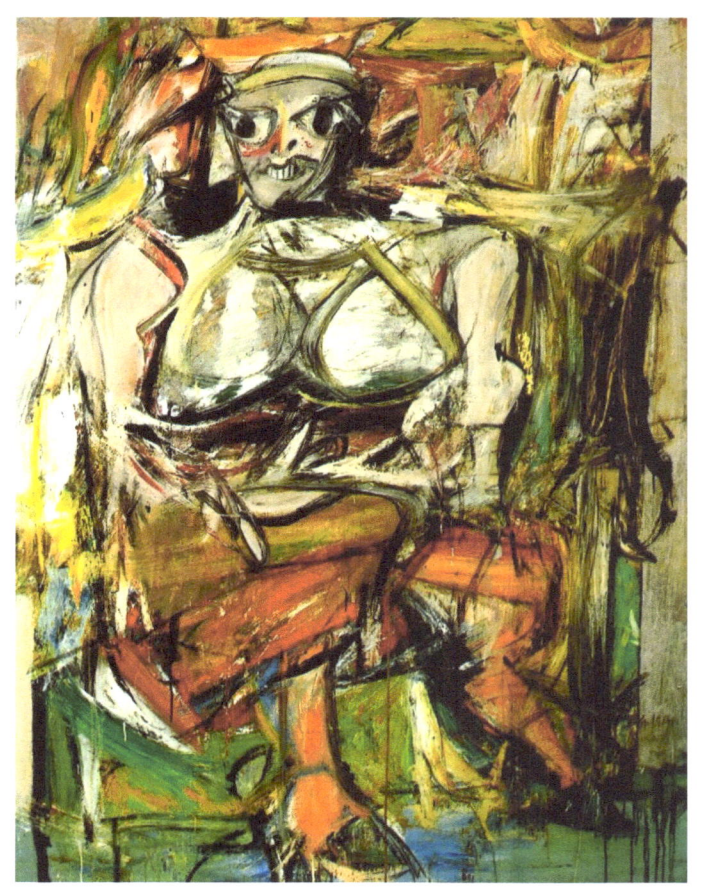

Williem de Kooning (1904-1997) was born in the Netherlands, but moved to New York at age 22. He was a prolific painter throughout his life. His work contains images of people depicted with rough cutting brushwork. De Kooning looked to express the his immediate personal experience. His monstrous paintings of women channel influences from stone age figures and from the artist's own mother. He once said, "All painting is an illusion. One idea is just as good as another it's what the artist does with the idea"

Williem de Kooning
Woman I
Oil on canvas 1950-52

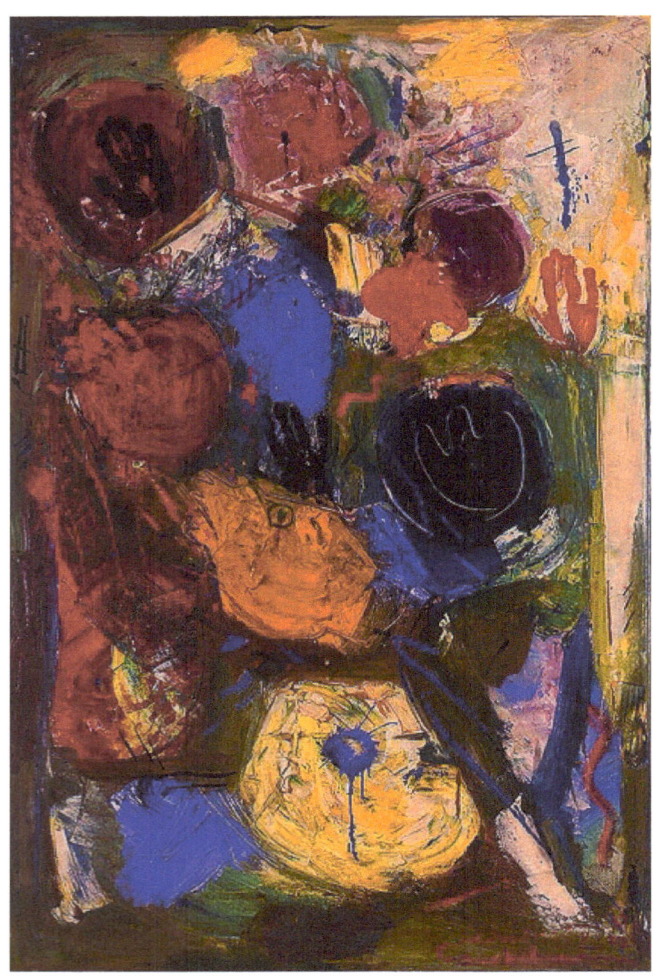

Hans Hoffman
Third Hand
oil on canvas 1947

Hans Hoffman (1880-1966) was a German born painter who moved to New York in 1932. He was important as both an artist and as a teacher to a generation of painters in both New York and Provincetown. Hoffman's idea of "push and pull" influenced the development of abstract painting for years to come. His artwork used color and shape to express what he called "inner necessity." The three handprints on his work *Third Hand* declare not only the physical presence of the artist, but the spiritual presence as well.

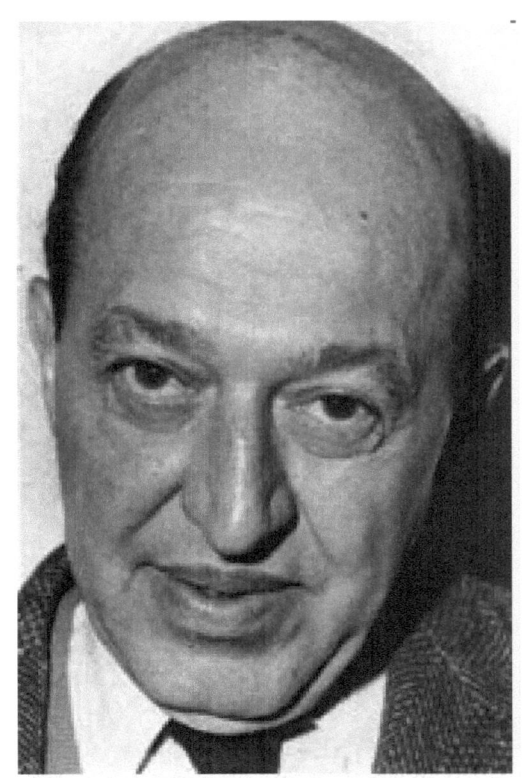

Clement Greenberg (1909-1994) was an American Art critic. His writings formed the basis of 20th century art theory after he rose to prominence with his essays "Avant Garde and Kitsch" and "Modernist Painting." He argued in favor of the growing Abstract Expressionist movement and American Art as the best in the world. He mainly praised the work for its commitment to flatness, a quality he saw as specific to the medium of paint. In his championing of the Abstract Expressionist painters, he often ignored the emotional and philosophical context in which the work was made. As time went on, he would become increasingly rigid in his opinions, leading to his fall from relevance.

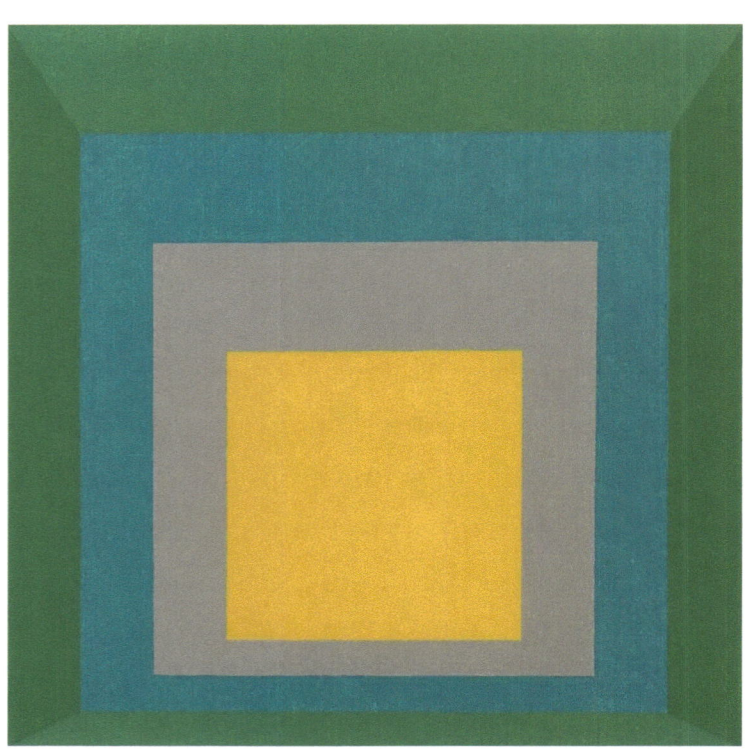

Josef Albers
Homage to the Square
Oil on Masonite 1959

Josef Albers (1888-1976) was a German born artist and faculty member at the Bauhaus School. He fled to the United States to escape the Nazi party. After moving to the U.S. he taught at Black Mountain College, an experimental art college in North Carolina. While there he challenged students to rigorously and scientifically explore their materials. He thought this exploration should "embrace all means opposing disorder and accident." This was in contrast to his colleague John Cage's embracement of chance.

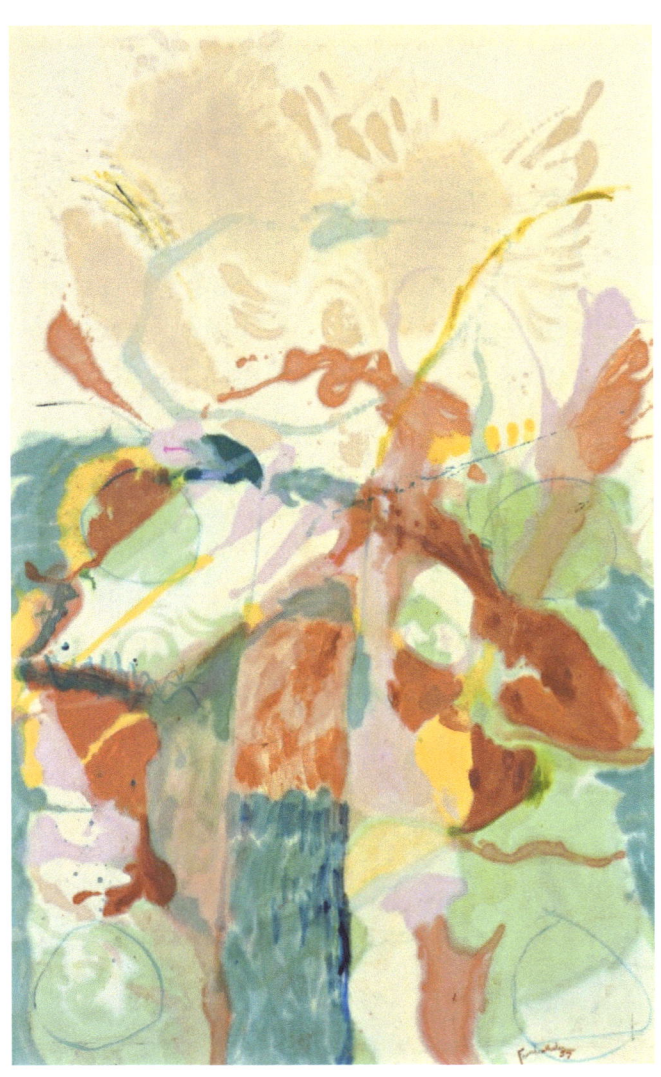

Helen Frankenthaler (1928-2011) was an American painter and printmaker, and one of the premier Color Field painters. Her work involved staining unprimed canvas with oil paint and creating overlapping forms. Her technique allowed the paint to soak into the fibers of the canvas creating an exceptionally flat surface that was celebrated by critic and close friend Clement Greenberg. In spite of the physical flatness of the surface, Frankenthaler's work displayed "tremendous perspective space despite the emphasis on flat surface"

Helen Frankenthaler
Jacob's Ladder
Oil on canvas 1957

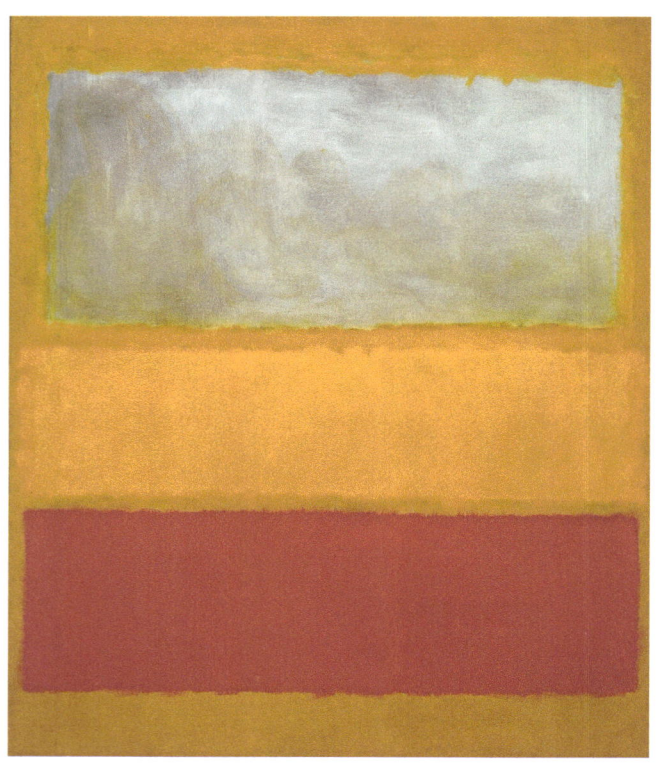

Mark Rothko 1903–1970 was an artist of Russian Jewish descent who lived and worked in New York. Throughout his life, Rothko struggled with his mental health. Rothko's work, in contrast to his contemporaries, challenged the viewer to sit with a piece in quiet contemplation. His broad bands of color at first seem quiet and still, but slowly begin to vibrate with nervous energy as they reveal subtle shifts in form and hue. In a letter to the New York Times he once called them "the simple expression of the complex thought and the impact of the unequivocal."

Mark Rothko
No. 13 (White, Red on Yellow)
oil on canvas 1958

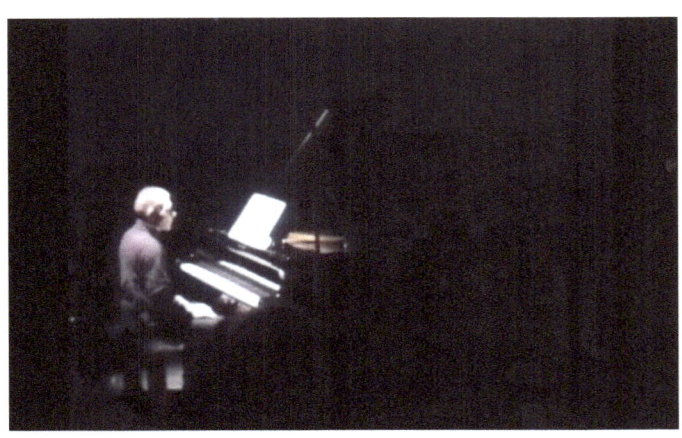

John Cage Performing 4'33" in 1952

John Cage (1912-1992) was an American composer and teacher at Black Mountain College. He laid the groundwork for modern dance, sound art, and performance art. Cage's interest in Eastern religion, particularly Zen Buddhism, lead him to investigate the potential of chance in art. He once stated that his "purpose was to remove purposes." His famous piece 4'33" consisted of a soloist entering and sitting at a piano for 4 minutes and 33 seconds without playing. The collection of coughs, creaking chairs and other random sounds that occur during the performance are treated as equal to the more refined sounds we traditionally consider music.

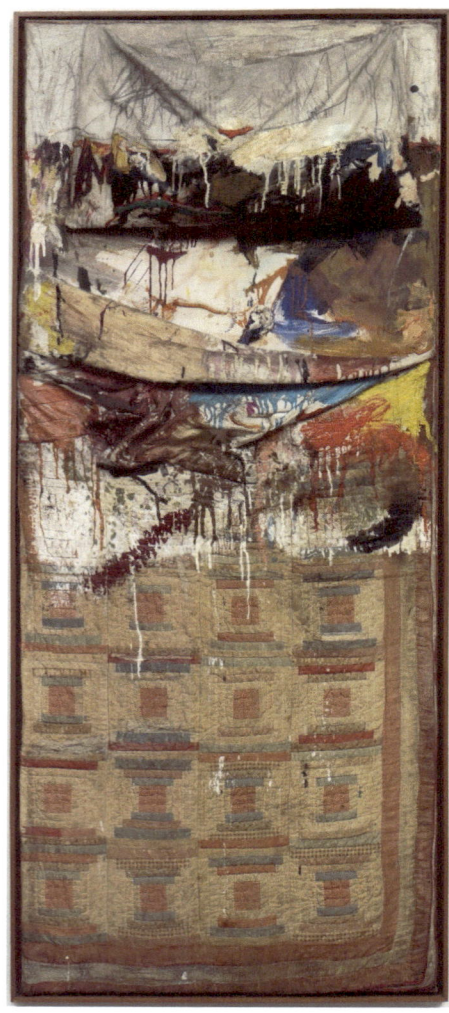

Robert Rauschenberg
Bed
Combine Painting: oil and pencil on pillow quilt and sheets on wood supports
1955

Robert Rauschenberg (1925 - 2008) was an American painter and sculptor born in Texas. After attending Black Mountain College, he moved to New York. Rauschenberg "reveled in the bewildering complexity of life." He made sculptural paintings he called "combines" in which objects (often found in garbage) were assembled and painted. He would later move into assembling found images though silkscreen. "When you realize the canvas you are painting on is simply another rag, then it doesn't matter if you use stuffed chickens or electric light bulbs"

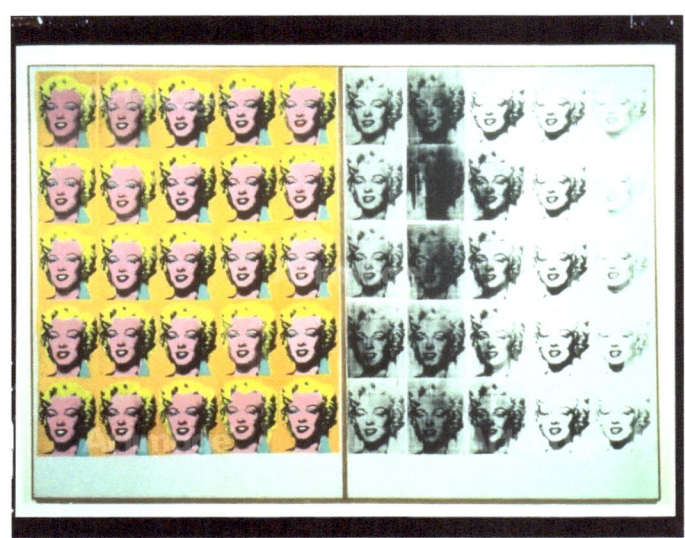

Andy Warhol (1928-1987) was an American painter and filmmaker. Andy was a pop culture icon whose work dealt with the artificiality of American culture and celebrity. His often blasé public persona belied a preoccupation with death. His work often repeated images that were at the same time glamourous and macabre. His famous quote "everyone will be famous for 15 minutes" hints at the temporary nature of life.

Andy Warhol
Marilyn Diptych
Synthetic Polymer Paint on Canvas 1962

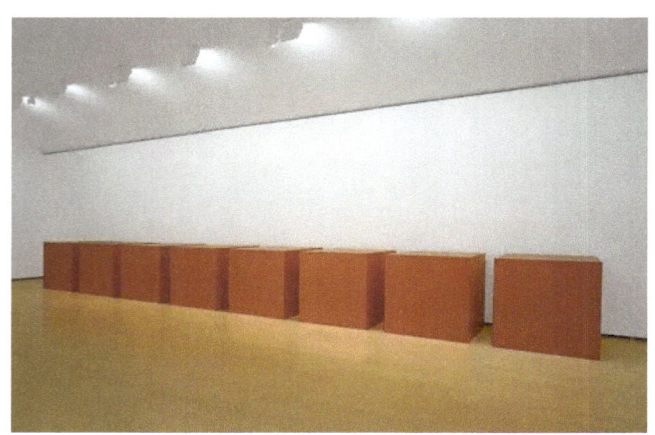

Donald Judd
Untitled
Orange enamel on cold-rolled steel, eight units with 12-inch intervals 1971

Donald Judd (1928-1994) was an American sculptor who lived and worked in New York. Judd abandoned painting to create repeated industrial shapes. He claimed his objects had no message outside of what was actually there without illusion or connection, "Real materials in real space" as he called them. The industrial and geometric perfection of his objects contrasted the random wildness of nature.

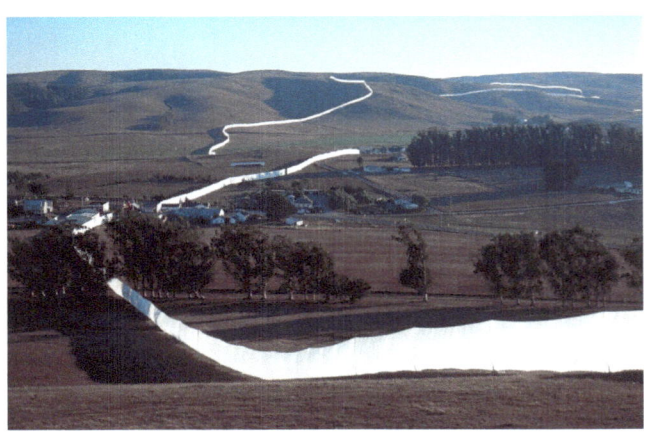

Christo and Jeanne Claude
Running Fence
24.5 miles of nylon fabric and steel posts
1977

Christo (1935-) **and Jeanne-Claude** (1935-2009) were a husband wife artist team that made several large scale temporary sculptures. Originally from Bulgaria and Morocco, Christo and Jeanne Claude created projects so massive in scale that they often took decades to complete. They considered every step of the process, from community meetings to fabrication, to be a part of the artwork. Each project is paid for through the sale of preparatory drawings and models. Their project Running Fence consisted of a 24.5 mile long fabric fence winding along the hills of Sonoma, California and into the Pacific Ocean for 2 weeks. It was met with mixed public support, but was completed when a court decided to not halt construction.

Works Cited

Burns, Ric, director. *Andy Warhol: A Documentary Film*. Steeplechase Films, 2006.

Díaz Eva. *The Experimenters: Chance and Design at Black Mountain College*. University of Chicago Press, 2014.

Fandrich, Leslie. *"New York in the 1940s and 1950s: Beneath the Surface." Massachusetts College of Art, Boston, Dec. 2016.*

Fineberg, Jonathan David. *Art Since 1940: Strategies of Being*. Laurence King, 2000.

Greenberg, Clement, and John O'Brian. *Modernism with a Vengeance: 1957-1969*. Univ. of Chicago Press, 1986.

"Marc Rothko: Reflection." Museum of Fine Arts, Boston.

Maysles, Albert, et al. *Running Fence*. Maysles Films, 1978.

Stiles, Kristine, and Peter Howard Selz. *Theories and Documents of Contemporary Art: A Sourcebook of Artists' Writings*. University of California Press, 1996.

www.ingramcontent.com/pod-product-compliance
Lightning Source LLC
Chambersburg PA
CBHW040453220526
45473CB00004B/1621